Feedback for Kathleen Emma's Work

"[Her writing seems] to revel in this kind of accumulation of objects and ideas that shouldn't necessarily be together, and a great sense of humor. [She has] such a strong voice, striking a tone that is world weary and sometimes slightly misanthropic but never too jaded to find moments of incredible beauty and humor, accepting the small victories with grace. [She has] a great eye for absurdity — and there's too much to keep track of these days." – J. O'Keefe

"This...has an old pulpy Charles Willeford feel – the land of used car lots, deco and grifters. Dialogue is great, cinematic and quick fire. Very entertaining to read! Also reminded me of a Confederacy of Dunces." – S. Kevorkian

"There is a softness to [her] writing. In letting go, she comes to terms with finding serenity in the imperfection. The [narration] meets the relationship with the self and with the other with grace, and it is a feeling that extends to the reader. I'm thankful for Kathleen's vulnerability and ability to articulate her raw experience so well." – E. Herrgott

"Truly, Kathleen's sentiments are so profound, each could stand alone, giving so much meat to ruminate on and consider, but of course they're made all the more thoughtful, poignant and pleasurable by how they come together. There is so much between the words left unsaid here, so many questions implied but not asked, and it really makes her words stay with me long after reading. I love the playful tone she brings to the meaningful subjects of her work — it's a pleasure to read." – K. Clark-Alsadder

"Kathleen has a true gift! There is something so true and pithy in the way she combines words and metaphors. I love her voice and really want to hear more of it! The first lines grab me straight away, she has a real talent for that." – O. Klinger

Safety Requires Avoiding Unnecessary Conversation

Kathleen Emma

Author's note: The events described in these stories are real. The
details are as best as I can remember them, capturing the spirit, if not
the actuality of the interactions.

Printed in the United States of America

FIRST PRINTING, 2019

ISBN 978-0-578-21851-9

Kathleen Emma
San Francisco, CA

kathleen@kathleenemma.com

"She lives in a San Francisco environment of very strange fantasies and very strange understandings of reality." - Newt Gingrich on Nancy Pelosi

Contents

49 Mile Scenic Meander: A Prologue of Sorts

With tears streaming down her face, a woman implores me to vote. "It's the easiest way we have to make impactful change. It's our responsibility to ourselves, and to each other." I sort of roll my eyes, but years later, I realize, I've become that woman. Suddenly, she doesn't seem so crazy.

It's a warm Sunday. I sit in the bus shelter at McAllister and Van Ness. A man wants my cell phone number. I say no, I don't have one. Barely a lie. "You're a white bitch in a box," he rages. Years later, I walk along 18th Street on my way to volunteer at the Women's Building, and another man looks me up and down and says, "Damn, you're too pretty to be a white girl."

I have rosé and lamb with a group of smart people, while feeling underqualified to talk about the latest on NPR. I discuss intellectual property and eat duck a L'Orange at a dinner that costs hundreds of dollars. I take my turn cooking Costco chicken so frequently that I think I've tried it every which way possible. Someone convinces me to try veganism, and I immediately regret it. I drink margaritas, and then attend a Seder meal where I swallow a big spoonful of raw horseradish for the first time. It's the "sting of the Jews," and I feel immediately guilty for all of the Christian privilege I've ever enjoyed. I celebrate a romantic accomplishment by eating chicken liver and am promptly struck with life-threatening food poisoning. I eat pizza, lots of pizza, and scarf down the best sandwich of my life. I sit on the street next to a homeless man in the Castro and we devour fresh-baked focaccia from my backpack. A woman gives me career advice over cherry pie, and we eat French fries at a diner where someone was murdered. I join a CSA and try every type of lettuce available. I still have no idea how to make mustard greens palatable. I drink all kinds of beer: basic beer, fancy one-of-a-kind beer, beer someone brewed in their garage. It all tastes the same after a while, but the memories turn into emotional tasting notes of sorts.

I run for a bus that I end up missing. A kind woman takes pity on me, tells me to hop in her car and drives me six blocks to catch it. I listen to an obscure band alone at the Hemlock, make friends with two older women, and at the end of the night they drive me home. Lesbian fairy godmothers all.

For months, I struggle to pay my rent and sell my $45 paper Muni pass for $42 outside a big, fancy office building, shocked by how many people on craigslist want to save three dollars. I star in an indie horror film and wear a heavy wooden mask in exchange for a free lunch. I watch a gunpoint robbery at Taqueria Vallarta, lose my appetite and give up my burrito. I have nothing but a $300 bed that a nice man sells to me. "You don't know what you want to do with your life?" he asks, as he dances dramatically around the store. "Don't worry, like a burlesque dancer, the universe will reveal itself to you," he tells me, fanning his face with an imaginary fan. I buy a mustard yellow damask print velvet armchair from woman named Squash in the Haight, and she throws in eleven mint green plastic tea cups for free. I drag a set of three white nesting tables onto the 38, to everyone's collective annoyance. I apply for hundreds of jobs to no avail. One day, I sit outside a skyscraper and cry into a voicemail, "I'm useless, no one wants me." Moments later, a woman sits next to me and holds my hand. "You'll be ok," she says. I get a job. I thank Craig, as if he's an extension of God, for making it all possible.

Liquor store owners show me how to break down Cornish game hens, teach me that Bounce dryer sheets prevent mosquito bites, and feed me the best homemade falafel and fluffy bread with Middle Eastern spices.

I'm up late, way too late, way too much, dancing into the night, pouring my heart out, waiting for busses and taxis that never come. I sing a lot, badly, until my voice is hoarse. Old men find this the most charming. A man who calls himself Mel Gibson offers to marry me if I promise to serenade him for the rest of his life. I politely decline.

For almost two decades, I feel safest within the confines of a single room, convincing myself that less space means less cleaning. I walk most everywhere.

I fall in love. Over and over. With bridges and people and concrete and dogs. With writers, poets, musicians and artists. With myself.

I start thinking of every challenge as a potential opportunity. My mind expands, my heart expands more. I'm covered in rain-fog mist, but I never feel cold.

I stand in the street protesting inequality, and celebrating small victories, however rare they may be. I realize that Northern California has made me soft and that I'm slowly turning into my own version of a San Francisco hippie liberal. I decide that I'm ok with that, even if it's meant as a disparagement outside of this magic, holographic-tinged bubble.

I stare at colorful houses out bus windows and I find myself in places I was told not to go. I look down from thousands of feet above and things seem peaceful and simple, even when I've made them impossibly complicated.

People come and go, I smile and I mourn. I long for days of the past and look forward to the future. The rain falls softly and, for once, everything is quiet.

The biggest park in the world is my backyard and I get rescued by Boy Scouts when my boat sinks in a shallow lake. I sleep in a mansion, in multiple offices, and in so many moldy rooms that I develop allergies. I spend three months looking at tiny apartments with Murphy beds and hot plates, wondering how anyone can survive without a window.

I ask questions that have no answers, but that doesn't stop me from searching. I become a regular, until I'm not. I realize that some things are better left preserved in the fossilized amber of time, and slowly let them go.

I find new ways to test my limits, and just when I think I've maxed out, I go further. I hang off the side of a cable car in busy traffic, convinced I'm going to die, but I don't. I give directions to a man who speaks only Korean and I help a grandmother find her way to the Apple store. She shows me selfies and close-up photos of flowers from the Japanese Tea Garden as we walk. Swaying at The Fillmore, I bump into another woman and say sorry. She tells me never to apologize for being present in the world. I cry.

I change empty toilet paper rolls in public bathrooms so often that I start joking to myself that it's the sole reason I was put on Earth. Sometimes when I'm lost, with no direction, it feels comforting.

I learn to step down, speak up, and question authority. Old architecture and graffiti murals give me hope. I jaywalk every morning, congratulating myself for doing something that scares me so early in the day. I wake up at 6:00 a.m. to pick confetti out of carpet and tell myself it will never happen again, but it does. Again and again and again.

Strangers hug me and grab my hands, hungry for human connection. There are some hungers food cannot allay. I come to know: we are all starving.

The Star Wars theme song drones endlessly from a busted birthday card and an old man wastes cracker crumbs feeding pigeons. Another time, I see a woman find a solitary broken boot on the ground and sell it to another woman. They haggle and finally land on a price: one dollar. These microscopic vignettes of humanity fuel me.

My mother taught me the golden rule of city living: don't make eye contact. Although I've tried, my curiosity has proven stronger than my willpower.

Safety may require avoiding unnecessary conversation, according to MUNI, but I learn that safety is merely an illusion.

A wizard touches my back and I wander down dark alleys. People grant me second, third and fourth chances I don't deserve, and are inexplicably patient with my inadequacy.

The teams I root for never win and we all wear black for days. Wind rushes through my hair and I fall off my bike in Golden Gate Park. I bruise, inside and out, but the scars mostly fade. I see things I never imagined, even in my wildest dreams, which are quite wild, even at their tamest.

I show strangers the most vulnerable parts of me and I learn to be honest. It feels good, even when it's hard.

The minute I leave, I feel my lifeblood drain, and the moment I return my equilibrium calibrates.

Orange lines crisscross against a bright blue backdrop and I remind myself that I have the best life. I raise my head toward the sky as I ascend the BART escalator, and I'm home.

Lulu

I can't stop staring at her forehead. Her voice is high-pitched, her blue eyes are lit with excitement and her hands gesticulate wildly, but her face shows no emotion. Not one muscle moves, not even just a little. The wonders of Botox.

"And now, let me show you the dresser," she chirps.

Down the hall we go as she patters on. "In case you were wondering, I went to a Botox party last night and I'm still a bit stuck!" I giggle politely.

She must have caught me looking.

We enter into a large spare bedroom, with an enormous mahogany dresser.

"Let me show you my favorite outfit!"

She pulls out a small fur cloak, with a sapphire and diamond brooch enclosure.

"It's real mink and the pin is real too, so be careful if you take her out in this one."

I am tempted to ask where one procures a mink coat for a dog, but not wanting to appear gauche, I'm instead left wondering what I've gotten myself into.

Lulu is a scraggly purebred Maltese show dog imported directly from France. She has seven long, unpronounceable names on her birth certificate and she cost $10,000.

I feel ill-equipped to be in her presence. In terms of pedigree, she is Lady and I am very much the Tramp.

She probably had ivory white fur at some point, but today it's more beige, with patches of light chocolate brown around her mouth and feet. Lulu looks like she recently frolicked in mud. "Some show dog," I think haughtily.

The tour of the Jackson Heights mansion continues and Lulu decides to join us.

Next up is the kitchen, which is furnished in designer gray and white swirled Italian marble ("Custom cut and flown in," according to Pamela). There are gorgeous state of the art appliances and a double oven. I mentally retreat, wondering who cooks and what they cook, but am pulled out of my thoughts when I hear her say that Lulu is fed hand-mixed, organic food and served water directly from the Brita filter, never the tap.

Of course Lulu is the one who enjoys the spoils of the most gorgeous kitchen I've ever seen. Am I comfortable grinding the food and mixing in the supplements? I pause before I answer. Am I? Without anything to qualify me, I have somehow become a house sitter, dog walker and personal chef (to a dog) in one fell swoop.

Lulu's dinner setup is akin to that of a Fancy Feast commercial, except real silver is involved, because of course. Plastic, with its potential BPA and carcinogenic qualities, would not suffice.

My shoulders start to feel itchy and I'm trapped in my own skin with anxious heat. If someone steals this dog, my life is over.

Trash gets taken out on Wednesdays, and I'm shown the most complicated washer-dryer combo, that future me would use and accidentally flood.

"Where are you headed?"

"We're traveling to St. Barths, and we usually bring her on trips but she hates the sand, which is why we're leaving her this time."

Lulu is perhaps the only creature I've ever encountered who would turn down a first-class, all-expenses paid trip to St. Barths because she dislikes sand.

Pamela leaves and I assure her, and sort of myself, that everything will be fine. Totally fine.

It's just me and Lulu now. Our time together starts off like an awkward first date. I'm out of her league, and she knows it. We don't have chemistry and she senses that I'm uncomfortable around her. Like most French citizens I've met, she's standoffish and thinks I'm an idiot.

I allow her to get in my head and it's perhaps the worst week of both of our lives.

I'm afraid that someone will steal her, so I barely walk her, only taking her out for five minutes a day. A few days in, I feel brave and guilty, and take her up to the park where she promptly runs away upon spotting a squirrel. "You are never leaving the house again," I manage to gasp once I finally catch her.

We head home and watch TV. Well, I watch TV. Lulu watches me intently, her head cocked to the side. "You're not getting anything," I say, as I accidentally spill beer on what I'm sure is a very expensive, custom-upholstered couch. She raises an eyebrow as if to let me know that she will be informing management of this encounter.

At night, we sleep in our separate gargantuan beds, however I cannot enjoy mine because Lulu cries and sighs all night, even when I scratch her head and plead with her to stop.

On our last night together, I apologize, and it feels like a weird breakup. Petting her between the ears, I tell her that I wish I could have been what she needed me to be, but I was scared. If something would have happened, I could never forgive myself.

She puts her head on my thigh and we sit in silence, both relieved that our short-lived relationship is coming to an end, relieved that our respective universes will soon be restored.

Cara

"Oh Lord! Whatever shall I order?"

A petite blonde woman in her early 30s sits at the breakfast counter at Brenda's and pores over the menu, periodically making "Mmmm mmmm mmmm" sounds in a Southern drawl.

"Ok, I think I got it! I will have the shrimp and grits, the beignet sampler—you get all four beignets, right?"

The waitress affirms this. "That's right. Chocolate, apple, plain and crawfish."

"Perfect, I will have that aaaaaaaand, what do you think? The hangtown fry or the French toast?"

"Depends on what you're looking for ma'am."

"Hmmm, well then, I will have the hangtown fry! Sounds exotic."

"Sure, coming right up."

The blonde turns her attention to the middle-aged man in a Hawaiian shirt sitting next to her.

"Howdy there, neighbor! I'm Cara from Houston. What's your name, darlin'?"

The man, clearly flattered by the attention, shakes her hand, "I'm Bob! I'm from Modesto."

"Oh, Modesto! That sounds interesting. Where is that?"

They engage in a long discussion involving what is and is not considered California's Central Valley, and before long, three enormous plates arrive in front of Cara.

"Oh, Lord! Look at all this food!"

"Aw come on, you're not gonna be able to eat all that, will you?"

"We'll see, Bob. We'll see," said Cara, gently touching his forearm while shaking her fork at him.

The two continue having a conversation entirely too ebullient for 8:00 a.m. on a Saturday morning, discussing all the things you shouldn't in polite company: religion, politics, sex, as she manages to completely demolish three huge plates of French soul food in under 20 minutes.

"You sure made a fool out of me! I've never seen anyone eat that much, that fast! I can barely finish my pancakes, and I've got 150 pounds on you!"

"Well, it was awfully delicious. It rivals the food my grandma used to make. I can see why this place is in all the guidebooks."

Cara dabs her lips daintily, and places her napkin to the side of her empty bowl of shrimp and grits.

"Bob, now that we're old friends, would you mind watching my things while I use the little ladies' room?"

"Of course, not a problem!"

Aside from the normal din of the restaurant, there is blissful silence for about five minutes.

Upon her return, the two of them continue talking as the waitress drops off the check. Cara reaches into her Louis Vuitton bag and suddenly her entire demeanor changes.

"Bob, you did watch my things while I used the restroom, didn't you?"

"Of course! No one touched anything."

"Oh no. This is not good. My wallet is missing. My wallet has been stolen!"

"Oh, come on, surely it has to be somewhere."

They look all over the bar and the floor to no avail. She checks her pockets. There is no wallet anywhere.

"Waitress, waitress! Yes. I have a problem. Someone in your establishment has stolen my wallet!"

"What? Are you sure? I didn't see anyone come in from outside."

"I am absolutely positive! I walked in with my wallet, and now it is missing!" She dramatically gestures at the rest of the patrons. "One of these derelicts must have stolen it while I was using the facilities!"

"Ok. Um, well. Let's check around. Maybe it fell out?"

In an act entirely outside of her job responsibilities, the waitress sweetly approaches every nearby patron and apologetically asks them to double check their personal belongings "just in case" a stray wallet had found its new home in someone else's bag.

In the meantime, Cara continues her campaign as a victim. "I demand to speak to the manager!"

The waitress goes to the back of the restaurant and comes back with a man in a bow tie. "This is Michael, he's our manager."

"I understand that you believe your wallet has been stolen, and that we've looked around and it doesn't appear to be anywhere?"

"That's right! Someone stole my wallet, and now, they refuse to give it back!"

"Ok ma'am, I understand that. We have made every effort to recover your wallet, but unfortunately, it does not appear that anyone has seen it or has it. The best I can suggest is that you file a police report. In the meantime, do you happen to have any other way to pay your check?"

"Are you kidding me? I've been robbed in your establishment and all you can think about is me paying a check?"

"Ma'am, I completely understand that, and I am truly sorry that your wallet has gone missing, but you did order, and eat, about $60 worth of food."

"Um, if it helps, I can pay the check," offers Bob.

"No, Bob! You should not have to pay for thievery! You keep your money! This entire thing is preposterous and I am not paying with money I don't have, from a wallet I don't have."

The entire restaurant is watching this scene play out, collectively wondering if, in accordance with restaurant lore, Cara will be put to work washing dishes.

The result is much less dramatic. Michael sighs deeply. "Well, if you don't have the money, you don't have the money. All I can ask is if you do find your wallet, that you try to pay the bill when you can. Other than that, good luck to you."

Cara's tone softens. "Well, I very much appreciate the consideration and your hospitality. I'm sorry that this otherwise lovely experience had to be tainted by theft."

She collects her things and turns to Bob. "Bob, what a pleasure meeting you. I hope you have a safe trip back to Modesto, and enjoy your daughter's volleyball game."

They hug.

Cara leaves the restaurant, as Michael and the waitress stare after her.

"I've never experienced anything like that," says the waitress, visibly shook.

"I haven't either. What a strange situation," says Michael.

Outside, Cara hails a cab and gets in.

"I wonder how she's going to pay for the cab," the waitress asks, still dazed.

There is silence for a moment until Michael slams his hand on the counter. "She's not! She's not going to pay for the cab! She's not going to pay us back! She didn't lose her wallet! She's a grifter! I cannot believe it!" He slams his hand down again.

"Clean up the plates, I don't want to see any trace of her."

Bob looks down at his still-unfinished pancakes as the waitress gathers up Cara's dishes. "But she was so nice," he says mournfully.

Vietnam Vet

Anyone have change for a fiver? Anyone have change for a fiver? For an old man? Anyone?

He makes his way to the back to of the bus, wearing jeans with bedazzled back pockets, a children's pink monkey backpack and a beanie.

Anyone have change for a VETERAN? A Vietnam vet? No? A purple heart Vietnam vet? I have bullet holes in my back!

The bus shifts awkwardly. Everyone pretends to be completely engrossed in their phones, books and hands, trying not to pay attention.

He takes a seat in the last row of the bus, unpaid.

We're going to have a good year next year. A really good year. The war is going to end.

*I'm a Vietnam vet...*he trails off. Then: tears, followed by deep, guttural sobs.

I went to war when I was 22. I killed a man. I killed my first man when I was 12. I didn't mean to. It was during a street gang fight in Milwaukee, Wisconsin. I killed him. Then I killed another man when I was 22 in the war. I killed a man.

And now I'm dying. Where's our healthcare, Obama? Us old people need our healthcare. We're dying. We need our healthcare. Where is the healthcare?

Obama needs to end the war. We need to get out of Afghanistan. Bring the boys home, Obama. Bring 'em home. Let them enjoy Christmas with their families. Come on, Obama. Please.

He gets up and wanders to the front of the bus, and faces the passengers.

I'm a special expert of demolition. You're in good hands. I could destroy a city if I needed to. Momma, I told you I'd make it home, Momma, I told you I would. Why couldn't you wait, Momma? Why'd you have to die?

He puts his head in his hands and sobs.

The bus driver stops the bus. She gets up out of her seat and pats him on the back. *It's going to be OK. It's going to be OK. Just sit down.*

I'm sorry bus driver, it's just a hard time. I'm sorry bus driver.

She walks back to her seat. The bus starts again.

The vet calms down for a moment. He turns to the woman next to him. *You're pretty. Really pretty.* The bus shifts awkwardly again.

Bring the boys home, Obama. Bring 'em home. Let 'em enjoy Christmas with their families. I'm sorry. It's just a hard time of year. I'm sorry.

Bus driver, do you think you can drop me off by the 7-Eleven?

He stands at the front, waiting to get off.

The bus pulls into the bus lane and he descends the steps.

I'm sorry bus driver, I'm really sorry.

k

The year is 2112 in a 10x10 room with low ceilings and exposed beams in a half unit basement in the Haight, filled with 20 bespectacled guys standing shoulder to shoulder, surrounded by a few six-foot-tall circuited machines and neon cords going every which way.

Lights blink on and off as robots attempt to speak, beeps and boops filling the air, which kind of smells like mold and cat pee and weed and patchouli.

With surgical precision, magicians push buttons, and voila, we have a new beat, a new melody is brought into the world.

Heads bob along, feet tap and hips sway. Turn down the testosterone and turn up the jams. Louder and louder until earplugs find themselves wheedled into eardrums, at about the time the bass drops.

How much of this is Frankenstein and how much is the monster? It's pre-recorded, but live, and I built it myself, with parts named Rosie and René, after Descartes, of course.

I think, therefore I am, but what about this modular geometry? And the cars that announce that they are driving themselves? Here's a message for your mouth: in the future there will be robots, and the future is now.

Hold on to saggy flesh while you can, and touch all the buttons you want, expressing the music in your mind. Because one day, someday soon, no one will ask whether or not you're a robot as a means of an identity check. Click click, welcome to the new order.

Fievel, Gus and Friends

There are many ways to kill a mouse.

Chase it all over; running, jumping around, cursing, before finally backing it into a corner and grabbing it, while twisting its neck and feeling its body go limp in your palm.

Rig up wooden traps with some cheese or peanut butter, and hope the mouse isn't tricky enough to eat the bait without being caught.

Get a cat and hope for the best.

Put down poison and wait for the mouse to gnaw through it, before getting sick and crawling into some hard-to-reach spot to eventually die and rot, starting a new plague with its deteriorating flesh.

Spray ammonia, plug up the holes with steel wool and then cover them with duct tape.

Or, torture yourself, and the mouse, and employ a glue trap.

The mice were around for about a month, but it felt like an eternity. The house guest no one wants. They crawled in through a very small hole in the corner of a random closet. "You can see the mouse grease on the wall," the exterminator told me, pointing out a sticky gray dust smear.

They ate through crafting supplies and any stray paper. They chewed the television cable and the phone lines. They pooped on the windowsills. At night, they hid in the walls, scratching and incessantly clawing.

When doors opened, they scattered across the room. The exterminator explained that typically mice stayed close to the baseboards since they were blind, but not these brazen rodents. In a power struggle between Davids and Goliaths, the Goliaths tiptoed around, living in constant fear of accidentally stepping on one and squashing it.

When explaining the anxiety of not knowing where mice might be hiding to an outsider, they usually minimize these feelings by saying something about how humans are so much bigger and how mice are so afraid of us, which is a nice, empathetic way to think about it. But it does nothing to alleviate the full body itch that comes from wondering when they'll appear next or if they're scampering across the bed as you sleep.

Ours was a mutual relationship of terrorism, and our household used every method available to try and eradicate their presence. At the time, living in a vermin deathtrap seemed normal, sane even. We didn't feel bad about how we tried to kill them, because it was only an idea, not a reality, until one day, one faulty footstep resulted in a glue trap mine ensnarement.

I came home from a long weekend to find a thumb-sized mouse with its tiny paws stuck in glue. A brief moment of emotional triumph was cut short as a closer look revealed a live mouse, struggling to get out. It was a baby, and it had vomited and defecated. It was scared, and sick, and helpless.

My stomach churned and my moral compass swiveled. The mice may have been a nuisance, but this was no excuse for violating my own standards of humanity. Although it had been us vs. them for weeks, the sticky trap non-death was not how I wanted to get rid of them. I didn't want them to suffer, I only wanted them gone. Hell, they could be alive, just be alive somewhere else.

Some things cannot be made right. And sometimes the most right thing still feels impossibly wrong, like wrapping a creature tightly in plastic and hoping it suffocates quickly.

Death may be forever, but compunction can feel that way too. Negative utilitarianism periodically haunts me. Who suffered more? The mouse or me? Was it necessary? Regardless, suffering is inevitable. Perhaps the real question has more to do with calculating the actual cost of causing another being to suffer so that we don't have to. Or whether technical wins can even be considered victories.

As much as our world would lead us to believe it, maybe not everything has to be a battle of who wins and who loses, of who dies and who lives. Coexistence is possible without cruelty, it's just a choice.

Into Space

We're hurtling through space at warp speed.

Ok, it's just Muni, it's probably more like 15 MPH and we're only going across the City, but it might as well be like we're jetting toward another planet.

We have limited food, water and air, subject to the throes of gravity, or at least brakes.

It's early, but we're ready. A vessel full of explorers on our way to conquer new lands.

Our team is comprised of mostly older Asian women clutching pink plastic bags.

In what shall now be known as a Chinatown baptism, the woman to my right smacks me in the head with a bag that smells like raw fish. It is fish. It is cold against my cheek. I am awakened.

Our captain is wearing a camo hat and doing a crossword puzzle. Everyone stays calm.

Diagonally across from me a man smokes a cigarette. No one stops him. Who would? Such blatant disregard for universally understood rules defies ordinary reprimand. You can get away with anything, until you're caught by someone bigger, stronger or more powerful. This I know.

Have you passed through this night? Another train speeds by.

A white guy with dreads juggles three lime green tennis balls. A man with huge sneakers and gold chains plays rap from a boombox that's at least 25 years old. A small child with pigtails blows a giant gum bubble that pops all over her face. A museum of oddity, all of us together, spanning time.

We all have different objectives, different missions. Suits, backpacks, yoga pants: the uniforms of explorers.

We slowly emerge from darkness. Life.

We could be anywhere, but here we are. In a new land. In a new world.

It's time to evacuate the capsule but there's a problem. The door won't open. We push the doors, we push each other. Finally, the solution comes like a chorus, "Step down!!"

Margo

"I only have one rule," she says.

Somehow, I don't believe her. I just spent an hour and a half signing a 60-page document, filled with rules and sub-rules.

No pets, not even a fish. Guests cannot stay longer than three consecutive days. Don't go on the roof. Don't paint. Don't be loud. You cannot hang pictures. Oh, by the way, there might be asbestos, and it might kill you, but you can't sue because you were forewarned. Please sign here and initial every page.

"My one rule is: don't jump on the fire escape."

I want to laugh, but instead I respond in all seriousness: "Oh. I think I can handle that."

"I had these two gals once, I don't know what they were doing, dancing? Anyway, they jumped so hard that the fire escape disconnected and it fell."

My jaw drops.

"Did they die?"

Her jaw drops.

"What? No! What kind of operation do you think I run? No, one gal broke her arm and the other one had some bruising. But you shouldn't do it, it's just a mess to deal with."

"Oh. Ok, I won't. Don't worry."

She shakes her head at me. "You have a wild imagination, don't you?"

Margo is maybe five feet tall, and that's in wedge flip flops. She has a shock of red-purple hair, that seems to be less of a stylistic decision and more of a circumstance, and she is wearing big bug-eyed sunglasses. We are indoors. She has kept them on during our whole two-hour-long meeting.

I don't really have anything to compare this to, but I'm pretty sure this is not how most lease signing meetings go. It's certainly not like my last lease signing, which consisted of me writing my name and number on a scrap of paper and handing it over to Wai Lee with a check. Those were the days.

I'm 27, and after almost 10 years of roommates, I want nothing more than to live alone. To have my own space. To not come home to a sink full of dishes I didn't use. I want to make the choice to not hear about someone else's day the minute I walk in the door. I want to buy nice stuff that I don't have to share.

I searched for months. Every weekend, I stood shoulder to shoulder with 40 other people, crammed into many tiny apartments, vying for a chance to shove my application into the landlord's hands. Frustratingly, there was always some girl who inexplicably managed to corner the landlord and snag the apartment on the spot. "Sorry everyone, the apartment's been rented!"

I saw apartments that I'm pretty sure were not real apartments, including a sub-level basement room without windows and a bathroom down a dark garage hall. I saw that apartment on my lunch break and one other guy showed up for the viewing. The landlord buzzed us in and told us to check it out ourselves, never bothering to greet us.

"Do you think this is safe to live in?" I asked him.

"Someone has definitely died here."

We left.

I upped my budget, convincing myself that freedom was priceless. I saw more places. I submitted countless applications and saved every penny to look like I was worth more than I was. I lived on craigslist, recognizing the apartments that never seemed to get rented. I was rejected, over and over. I decided that when I found a place, I would never move. I lowered my standards, and then lowered them some more, eventually raising them again.

One day, I saw the most beautiful apartment, better than anything I had seen throughout my entire search. It was bright, with classic San Francisco details, and huge windows looking out to the Bay. I did my best to ignore Ann, the building's manager, as she rummaged through the current tenant's dresser.

"I've been thinking of getting a dresser like this," she told me.

I submitted my application. I sent check copies, bank statements, pay stubs and a reference letter. And then, the most magical thing happened: the apartment was mine, which is how I came to be sitting there with Margo that day.

I arrived at an old Victorian in the Marina, surprised to find that it was set up like an office, rather than a house.

"Here's my lease. I signed every page," I said, handing her a copy.

"Oh, I'm going to have you sign another one. We're going to read through it together."

What she really meant was that she was going to read it to me, but not before taking a 15-minute break to talk to her best friend on speakerphone.

"Diannnnnne, Hawaii will be a total blast, won't it darling?"

They throw around superlatives and Margo comes up with a brilliant idea.

"Let's have code names on the trip!"

"Oooooooh! You can be Goldie LaMarge and I'll be Diane Coco!"

This continues as if I'm not there until Margo finally says, "Listen, I have this sweet girl in front of me waiting to sign her lease. I've got to go. Ciao, darling!"

I soon learn that Margo signs off saying "Ciao," usually in caps lock, in every email, as she reminds us to never flush tampons and to always lock the doors.

We finally get through the lease, and the second most magical moment comes: she hands me the keys.

"Ok, well that's that. Have fun, be safe, and remember the number one rule. Repeat after me: I will not jump on the fire escape."

"I will not jump on the fire escape," I repeat solemnly.

Joan

The smell. It's cement, with mold, with a breeze, with apartment dust and bus exhaust. It's my grandparents' basement in Queens 28 years ago. I haven't smelled it anywhere but there, but now it's here, following me.

Second floor. A refrigerator is in the hallway to the left, just off the stairway. A sign taped to the fridge reads in all caps: "SAVE MOVE TO CORNER OF LIVING ROOM COVER WITH PLASTIC!" Strange directions, but I would expect nothing less in the renovation of Joan's apartment.

In the lobby, at the mailbox bank. The box next to mine reads "McCormick" but some animal scratched it out months ago. It's the scratch out of a child who has made a spelling mistake, not the thick, dark, felt-tipped, single-lined Sharpied finality of death.

The corner of an envelope peeks out of the space between our mailboxes. I shut my door and wish I could empty its contents.

In death, as in life, Joan is ever present.

Over 30 people live in the ballerina pink, Victorian apartment building that is 820 Jones, but Joan was the only person I've ever really seen. She had lived in the building for a long time, at least long enough to be grandfathered in to legally smoke cigarettes in her unit.

I smelled her constantly and ran into her frequently, usually on Thursday nights when we both tried to do laundry. She would leave her laundry in 40 minutes past its expiration and I would seethe, a younger, less patient version of myself not understanding how anyone could violate the unspoken laws of social conduct so flagrantly.

One day, we ran into each other as I wrote passive aggressive notes in my mind. "Thursdays are my day to do laundry," she informed me matter-of-factly. "I put my sheets in and then call my friend."

"Oh, ok," I said, accepting her reality as a rule.

She changed the subject. "Isn't Ann a bitch?"

Ann, my across-the-hall neighbor, a thorn in my side, our building manager, my protector from Margo.

I had enough interactions with Ann over the years to entertain a gamut of possibilities of her schema ranging from she's a bitch to she's just artistic to she's on the spectrum. I firmly believe that she is fine and well-intentioned and a touch socially awkward, but I could understand why Joan hated her.

Diplomatically, I half-heartedly agreed, "She can be."

Joan nodded in approval.

"Remember, Thursdays are my day and I do three loads."

"You got it."

Eventually I got tired of waiting for her to take her laundry out and switched up my schedule. We still ran into each other often though. We'd say hi and she'd always have something to say about Ann. I would always smell the nauseating scent of cigarettes on my way down the stairs.

The last time I saw Joan, she had a walker that she was unsuccessfully trying to maneuver into the double gated vintage elevator. I grabbed the outside door and she snarled, "I don't need help from anyone!" I let her go.

Weeks later, the residents of the building received an email from Margo titled "820 Jones sad news," which read:

Sad news.

Several of you saw the police activity in the building. They were there because one of the residents, Joan, passed away. One of the residents called me this morning expressing concern because she had not heard from Joan in a long time. She asked me to investigate, and after hearing from several other residents saying they had not heard from Joan, I called the police. The police found her. They have locked down her apartment.

Joan lived in the building for a long time and was friendly with the residents that lived around her.

She was a tennis player and loved watching tennis. Rest in peace Joan.

Ciao Margo

It was strange in her passing to find out this new information about tennis. To me, she had always just been a woman who enjoyed cigarettes and clean sheets.

Caution tape lined her door frame for weeks, a strange memorial.

We're here, until we're not. I learn this over and over, but it's a new lesson every time. Change is a constant, but nothing makes me feel so vulnerable as the moment when something morphs from one thing to the next. The alchemy of presence, of physical form, to distant memory.

I knew the day would come when McCormick would disappear entirely off the mailbox, but I didn't anticipate that it would be today. The childish scrawl has been replaced by empty blackness.

Eventually, change strikes the mailbox again. And just like that: Kelly.

Logan

"Adoo-doo, adoo-day! Hillary Clinton! Donald Trump! BIDEN SAVE US!!! Adoo-doo, adoo-day!"

This fucking guy again.

It's 4:00 a.m., and I just fell asleep an hour and a half ago.

I don't always have insomnia, but when I do, it plagues me for weeks on end. It becomes a routine. A routine, just like this guy who insists on spouting gibberish at the top of his lungs as he marches up Jones Street every morning for the last three months.

Gibberish. I got in trouble for using that word online in our neighborhood group.

Drew Simpson: "What you call 'gibberish' — perhaps is it just a language you don't understand?"

Fuck you, Drew. I haven't slept in weeks and all you can worry about is if I'm using the right PC term for psychotic ranting? Fuck you.

The comical guideline in San Francisco real estate is to make a list of your top five "must haves" and then cross out three. When I moved Downtown, it was with the understanding that noise and crime came with the neighborhood. Cheap rent and walkability have tradeoffs.

But this, this is too much.

"The abyss" is the name I've given this purgatorial space between sleep and waking life, a nightly storm of swirling thoughts and worst-case scenarios, robbing me of my sanity and any semblance of higher-level functionality. I feel how the addicts on Ellis and Jones look: zombied and strung out. When I can finally quiet myself long enough to reset, I'm woken by what feels like a sick joke. There's nowhere I can go to escape our political inevitability. Not even my sleep.

I lie awake and wonder about this man. Why is he doing this? Psychiatric duress? Is he an insomniac too? Is it an Ambien haze? Performance art? An act of political resistance? Is he trying to literally wake the masses and force us to confront the sins of our past voting records? It doesn't matter because there is no answer, but I democratically try to consider the options, rather than indulging the rage boiling up inside of me.

But who says one man can't change the world? Joe Biden's biggest frenemy's rants have had an unintended side effect in that the Tendernob has come together to find a solution. We've all called the cops, but after flooding the non-emergency line with countless early morning phone calls, it's been determined that there's nothing they can do. Did you know that you can't arrest someone for public disturbance if they're moving?

The women that answer the non-emergency line are patient. "What is he wearing? What direction is he heading?" they ask.

It's 4:00 a.m. again and my sleep-estranged brain spins. "North? Now he's making a right? He's wearing a brown sweatshirt, I think." It takes every fiber of my being not to break down in a tantrum. I want to cry. Please, fix it. Make him stop.

"I'm sorry this is happening, but there is not much we can do. We'll try to send a car."

We've tried everything. We've filmed him, we've taken pictures, people have approached him on the sidewalk, others yell out their windows, begging him to be quiet. In an act I'm not sure if I find heroic or insane, one neighbor followed him on the bus to his workplace. His name is Logan and he works at a restaurant in Japantown. At work he is apparently normal, which only confuses me more. What is this double life?

Since the cops are of no help, the neighbors share different philosophies of how to obtain vigilante justice and reclaim our sleep. Some people suggest that he's mentally ill and needs help. "That much is clear!" the sleep-deprived among us exclaim. Tough guys threaten to beat him up. There's talk of pepper spray, fists and guns. Crazy begets crazy. Someone posts Logan's apartment address and others tell stories of approaching him in the street. Secret side groups emerge for those who don't feel as if the public group is accomplishing enough. Sometimes, the trolls come out, which would amuse me if I weren't so exhausted. We're being trolled regardless. One guy says he knows the police chief and has organized a meeting. The police chief is getting involved? For one guy who causes a disruption for maybe thirty minutes a day? Suddenly, our collective loss of sleep feels so small in the context of larger city crimes and issues.

The truth is that it's difficult to live in harmony with mental illness. You tackle it or you learn to ignore it. Those are the options.

Watching my neighbors come together to figure this out has, in a very minute way, made me feel like anything is possible when people work together to achieve a goal. I've come to see the aural terrorism on Jones Street as an allegory for what's happening in our world and in our country. There are problems, and there are solutions. The solutions seem clear depending on your perspective.

But really, what I've come to know is that the line between sanity and insanity is razor thin. It's the difference between two hours of sleep and four, the anonymity of the street and the safe harbor of the familiar, of meds and no meds.

Adoo-doo, adoo-day.

Sonic Poisoning

Darkness, illuminated by a tiny light.

Diamonds all around, if you just know where to look.

A cacophony of Cheetos, bug out bags, Tide pods, non-stop viral videos and pussy hats litter the scene.

Is there a mute button? Who picks up the trash in this exhausting world?

Deeper I wander, searching for quiet.

Searching for a place with no needs or wants or timelines. Or voicemail. Or email.

Time stands still on a bus that struggles up the hill in Bernal Heights.

There is laughing and green grass and treacherous turns, a temporary escape.

The most important question becomes: will the bus sideswipe a minivan?

It doesn't, and no one seems to notice, instead, taking for granted the micro-movements that need to occur for safety to remain an undervalued resource.

It's dark and silent where I'm going, a dive bar in the middle of the day, until other people show up and ruin that too.

Things are still in the back of a taxi cab where the driver doesn't pollute the space with extroversion.

I seek out places devoid of humans, but always, there is a cough or a rustle, and usually a horn or a siren. Always a horn or a siren.

Even sign language seems loud when signers yell.

The best is being outside when it's raining softly, when the droplets fall and muffle the sound of everything.

The trolley gets going, and for a while, until Powell, it's my own private chauffeured ride down Market Street. The best two dollars I've ever spent.

I walk down a deserted alley, while the whole world has gone to sleep, just to feel as if something is all mine, just for a moment.

Taking an elevator ride alone is rare, but always feels like getting away with something. Sometimes I spin around and dance, hoping I'm not being secretly watched.

Running for a stretch, without having to bob or duck or stay to the right, is freedom.

Solitude feels impossible when connection is constant, so I'm grateful for the rare moments when the girl in the apartment above isn't stomping around.

How strange, my phone has no bars, which feels so much more delicious than it should.

Descending a few flights of stairs into mildewed darkness, I am Ponce de Leon, lost amidst dusty old books, where language is dead and my gold is silence.

The 38

At the corner of Ninth and Geary, a growling pit bull wearing a spiked collar, and his owner, a scraggly grunting chain smoker with giant headphones, wait for the 38 headed inbound.

When the bus eventually pulls up, the pair head to the last row. The bus scoots along until it halts to an abrupt stop at Geary and Spruce, where the bus driver yells, "PUT A MUZZLE ON THE DOG!"

Confusion abounds, with everyone looking around to see who he is addressing.

Thirty seconds later, the bus driver, bearing a striking resemblance to peak weight Mr. T, storms to the back of the bus with a briefcase. "PUT A MUZZLE ON THE DOG!"

The bus driver towers over the dog owner, who finally looks up and says, "What man? I can't hear you, I have my headphones on."

A man in the front, staring intently toward the back of the bus starts providing a play-by-play for the other passengers. "Despite repeated warnings, it appears as if the muzzle IS STILL NOT on the dog!"

Exasperated, the bus driver raises the briefcase over his head and repeats himself. "You put the muzzle on the dog, or I'll throw you off the bus!"

"Oh, fuck that, man. I'm not doing shit."

"OK, that's IT! You used profanity, GET OFF THE BUS!"

More cursing ensues until the dog owner finally exits the bus and tells the driver, "I'll see you outside!" to which the bus driver responds, "Son, you don't want to see me outside!"

The unofficial bus spokesman continues his update in a voice typically reserved for football upsets, "Update! The man with the dog has now been THROWN OFF THE BUS!"

The bus driver makes his way back up to the front, apologizing to everyone as he passes.

Our public transit announcer takes the opportunity to address the bus driver. "It's ok, bus driver, you don't have to be afraid of that guy. Thanks for doing your job."

The bus revs as the guy with the dog reappears at the front, yelling something barely audible from inside the bus, provoking the driver to open the door to yell, "I think you have me confused with YOUR MOTHER!"

Defending his mother's honor, the dog owner responds, "I'm gonna kill YOU!" Without skipping a beat, the bus driver trumps him saying, "I'll kill YOU AND YOUR DOG!" and shuts the door as the bus starts to pull away.

Suddenly, there is a massive crash. The man with the dog threw his skateboard at the front door and the glass shattered completely.

Our narrator, clearly panicked, puts his hands out and says, "Ok, nobody panic. It appears that there is trouble on the bus. I REPEAT, TROUBLE ON THE BUS."

The driver gets on the announcement system and says, "Sorry folks, everyone needs to get off the bus. I need to wait for a supervisor."

The narrator stands up and continues explaining the whole situation saying, "Does everyone understand? There's been some trouble on the bus and we all need to get off. I repeat, trouble on the bus."

The bus is alive with murmurs, everyone shocked at the turn of events, as we exit single file. Another passenger shrugs and justifies the situation, "Well, he did say that he'd kill him AND his dog."

R.

I never thought I would threaten a suicidal person with murder, but all relationships have gray areas, I guess.

Ours exists somewhere between colleague and friend, of untrained psychologist and patient.

It's sandwiched between mixing the mundane with the existential, its own unique form of multitasking, a skill at which I've become particularly adept.

We have these long conversations, he and I. One moment we're navigating the intricacies of forwarding an email, the next we're delving into the depths of our confused existences.

For a while, the conversations were mostly me half-heartedly talking him out of suicide.

Conventional wisdom says that you should encourage people to live, to work through things.

"I'm 79, my wife left me, she took all my money and she ruined my life. What do I have to live for?"

He has a point.

I think of all the days that have been so hard for me to wake up and plug along, days where I've asked the same question.

So, I don't know how to lie and say, "But you have so much to live for!"

This has been going on for more than two years now. I thought it would get easier, that the pain would fade, but it mostly it's a roller coaster, full of ups and downs.

I thought the loss would dissipate over time. But I know now that loss doesn't ever really go away, it just transforms.

I know now that I said the wrong thing when he asked me if people remember us when we die.

"I think people remember us for the first couple of months, but then they get caught up in life's minutiae and slowly they forget, until they stop thinking of us at all."

He was afraid I was right. But I was not right.

He has the suicide planned out. There won't be a funeral. Maybe there will be a small memorial service, and if there is, only about 20 people, including me, can attend. I feel honored.

I forgot that philosophical conversations about suicide are not commonplace until one day when I received a call at the office from a very upset man.

"Do you work with R.?"

"Yes, I do. How can I help you?"

"Ok, so my brother had him in a casual carpool this morning and he was real shaken up by the conversation."

"Oh?"

"You do know what's going on with him, right?"

Oh God, what do I say?

"Um, yes."

"Well, aren't you worried?"

"Divorce can be a very traumatic experience," I hear myself say.

"My brother is going to call the cops so they can perform a wellness check."

Oh no.

"Oh. Well. I'm not sure that's completely necessary. He's on his way to the office."

"Do you promise you'll check on him? My brother is very worried and asked me to call someone. He's pretty sure he's in danger."

"I promise. Thank you for your call, and thank your brother too."

Moments later, "Hey, kiddo."

It's one thing for us to expose our darkness to people who can handle it, who are familiar with it, but we have a responsibility to know the boundaries of our own toxicity.

"If you don't kill yourself first, I will! You cannot keep telling people you are going to commit suicide! Especially not in casual carpool! It's supposed to be casual! Keep it light!"

It you wait long enough, and you do what you need to do, everything can get a little better in time.

We've come to a point where we rage against the machine, and make jokes at the expense of our demons.

After a particularly rough morning, I tell him that I have a theory that we're actually in Hell. He's thrilled. "Now things are getting interesting!" He refers to his divorce payments as a tribute, and I think we both walk away better for our respective absurd interpretations of reality.

Another day, we lament the uncertainty of progress due to the instability of our administration. "I fought for justice my whole life, and I thought I made a difference in the '60s and '70s, and throughout my career, advancing the state of the world. It's so hard to think that it was all for nothing. It's a really hard thought to sit with."

But on the best day, he tells me, "I don't want to kill myself as much anymore. I'm a little happier. I still don't know what I'm going to do with my life, but I'll figure it out."

"I am happy to hear that! You do sound better. And who ever knows what they're going to do with their life?"

"I don't know, but I think I'm going to stick around and see how things go."

1.

We could listen to country music for liberals
Or watch the government shock and awe us with a 9/11 throwback,
But instead we lie on the floor, letting a baby feed us imaginary food
And it feels good to have a break from the discordance.

It's impossible to tell if a man is facing you, or if his back is to you.
It doesn't matter much though, because abstraction is its own form of
decadence,
In the same way that it feels good not to poach your own eggs or cook
your own bacon.
There's luxury in being taken care of,
And that's a trueism you can take to the bank.

I'm in Italy, having dinner with the sister I never had,
Before we transport to see The Queen perform in front of other queens,
who have glitter smeared across their cheeks.
It makes us feel good to see that there is still room in the world for 47-
year-old women whipping their hair,
And being whomever you please,
Even when it feels like everything is against us.

A bus trudges up a narrow road, navigating between tiny houses and
lots of trees, and I might be on Capri on my way to see Tiberius,
Or I might not,
But either way, it feels serendipitous to climb 37 steps to see a view
that has been around for 85 years as of today, the day I'm seeing it for
the first time,
And I owe something, a lot of things, to a woman who smoked cigars
and drank scotch and wore pants and fought fires, which I do almost
never, but sometimes, most every day, and constantly.

I stop into a house run by men, to kneel in front of a woman
And thank her for other women,
Especially the ones that aren't here anymore.

A sign warns me not to ask for what I want,
So I don't,
But I'm still a little disappointed when the thing I want becomes available
The second after I say what I'll accept as its substitute.

It's too much cheese, says the man in the explorer hat.
I'm sorry?
It's too much cheese!
In the moment, I affirm him, but later it becomes a joke: emotionally lactose intolerant.

A violin starts and stops until it stops for good and I wonder where it went.
Directions pass by me: Drink Russian, Drive German, Wear Italian, Kiss French.
There is truly something for everyone in this strange world.

I try to solve a mystery.
Who is Cyrus?
A smiling man is gone, but omnipresent.

I take a step back in time
And feel like an outsider looking in.
I'm not a Beat poet, but maybe in another lifetime, I could be.
There's talk of Rodin
And someone says, "I've got a damn good forgetance"
Which is like remembrance, but the other way around.
A hippie with a cell phone is a funny sight.

I find a silly deal in Chinatown,
And I'm pretty sure I'm getting ripped off
But I'm not mad.
One elbow grips an armful of puppies
And the other holds on to a cable car for dear life.
Don't fall off.

2.

We're off to see the wizard,
But life imitates art
And it's a bit of a letdown,
Except for the part where we learn something new about ourselves.

I stare out the window in Lisbon,
Catching a sunburn
While a fat, fuzzy bumble bee wanders over.
And I'm scared,
Until I remember they don't sting,
Unless I'm misremembering that fact.
Be still, you are the bee, there is no need to panic, I tell myself.

There is pushing
And space negotiation.
Everyone lost as we lurch forward and stop short.
Where is anyone ever headed?

You can't go faster than what's in front of you
Is what a Camry learns
And I hope the woman
Who pushed me while I was waiting for a man with a walker to take a
big step down.

I'm in Thailand with a guy who says, "Bless" sincerely and is trying to
be his best self.
We talk about flexibility.
Both secretly glad we are learning to make micro-adjustments in our
framework,
Happy to have seen the Ghost of Christmas Future before it became our
reality.

Can I ask you a weird question?
You can, but only if you commit.
But I guess weird is subjective,
The way I think having an eyelid tattoo is certainly a choice, but I
would never blink at sharing a piece of paper.

Don't shit on my doorstep and call it art.

You're not The Most Famous Artist and this is not social commentary.
The rules change based on whether or not you know better,
But please don't infringe on my thought agency
In your chameleon echo chamber.

In a Haus that's unlike Olive Garden
A man sits at the head of the table,
Refusing to believe we are family.
I'm going to make my mess.
As if we ever asked him not to,
As if family wouldn't expect you to.

Old men express their anger so publicly,
Banging tables and waving their arms and storming back and forth.
What is that like?

Jehovah's Witnesses stand around
And follow me with their eyes.
Would you like to take a stress test now that your blood pressure is up?
Isn't heaven full yet?

You're only as cold as you think you feel,
I try to convince myself as mist assaults me like tiny bullets,
A baptism of sorts, the result of my own willful stupidity.

Home is surreal with trappings of real
Where I can be my acoustic self
Even when I'm only at 30% battery.
Cat Power fuels Ann Powers fuels me.

3.

I'm lost even though I know approximately where I'm going.
It's hot and cold and destabilizing,
But this is what needs to happen
So a Korean woman in Japantown
Can erase me.

I'm awake and attempting astral projection.
Transcend, you are outside of the pain.

Is this really the lesson you want to teach your children?
To evacuate in the midst of vulnerability?
It's been a long time since anyone wrapped me in a towel and rubbed my shoulders
But it feels like love.
An effusive woman wants to process
And somehow that feels so much more personal
But I do that too,
I'm Stretch Armstrong.

In a cross-town Venn diagram, a baby making funny faces is the common denominator
Between a Chinese grandma, a Mexican nanny and a woman on meth.
And I'd like to buy the world a Coke,
But apparently all anyone needs is someone cute to love,
Because that's the universal language.

Self-preservation sometimes means considering what's best for your future self
And now I'm Zen enough to know that.

Sitting with the silence al fresco
Is ok.
Rosie has arrived to clean up the mess,
But the robots we need don't exist quite yet.

The neighborhood is the same, but everything familiar is gone.
Remember kids, heroes get remembered, but legends never die.
God, and they're such kids, in their cult garb,
Walking brand marketing for the religion of Steve Jobs.
Take me to your leader,
And tell him to quit it with the updates, because now I can't figure out how my tether works.

Two men dig through an old can of nuts, the non-edible kind,
To find the right piece to take pictures in the past.
It's sweet, the way they emote over a time long gone.
But best of all, is that one of them never removes his bike helmet,
A flux capacitor for the brain.

San Francisco has a Venice Beach, and it feels nice to be around the similarly coiffed.

It's the simple pleasures,
Like a tiny bathroom covered in terrible graffiti and even happier hour.

Though I don't know what could be happier than an Indian summer
that cooperates,
And live music,
And chasing your bliss,
And a parklet full of puppies,
Sniffing each other out and deciding that everything is cool.

You're a spiritual being,
Exploring different eras.
Is the KitTea Cafe amazing or gross?
Both.
You get five stars.

Alan

"Rachel? Oh my God, Rachel, is that you?"

I look up. I am not Rachel, but I am interested in witnessing a potential long-lost reunion.

To our mutual disappointment, there is no reunion, because the voice was speaking to me, and I am Kathleen, and it's 8:00 a.m., and I'm just waiting for the bus because it's too cold to walk.

"Wow, I really thought you were my old girlfriend. I haven't seen her in 50 years," says the short, smartly-dressed, mid-70s aged man standing in front of me.

I'm constantly mistaken as younger than I really am, and I've never been mistaken for over 50, so I decide that a senile grandfather is on the loose.

"Oh, no worries," I say.

"You're not related to a Rachel, are you? Maybe a grandmother?"

"No, only an Evelyn and an Eileen."

"Where are they from?"

"New York, originally."

"You don't say! I'm from New York—Brooklyn!"

"Oh cool, part of my family is from Brooklyn too."

The man shakes his head and smiles. "What a coincidence to run into you today. I'm Alan."

I shake his outstretched hand. "Kathleen."

Alan tips his fedora and does sort of a half curtsy. "What a pleasure. Kismet, even." He is silent for a few moments as he stares off into the distance. I stare at my feet.

"Kathleen, meeting you today is making me think about what a wonderful life I've had."

"Oh, that's sweet, thank you."

"I was really lucky growing up, surrounded by good people and my family never wanted for money. You ever hear of Meyer Lansky?"

"The mob boss?"

"Everyone *always* thinks that. He owned half of Vegas, and was best friends with Sinatra. Get this—I was partially raised by the Rat Pack! I would go to all of their performances and hang out in their dressing rooms. That's where I learned how to sing."

He belts out a shaky rendition of the first few lines of "Fly Me to the Moon" and takes a deep bow.

"Wow, that must have been an interesting childhood."

"Well, you know, they were all part of the tribe too. We gotta stick together. You're Jewish—you know that."

"Oh, no, I'm not...I'm not Jewish."

"Oh." For a moment, Alan looks very disappointed.

"Well, that's ok. You're very nice anyway."

"Oh, uh, thank you."

There's an awkward silence and Alan is staring at his feet, so I step out into the street to look for the bus. *I probably should have just walked*, I think to myself.

Alan looks up at me, and his tone turns serious. "You know, since I grew up so well off, charity has always been very important to me. Even now. That's what I'm doing today. Three times a week I drive down from Calistoga and hand out sandwiches at GLIDE. I make about 800 sandwiches a week and give out 10,000 pairs of socks a year."

"Wow, that's amazing. That's terrific that you do that. So many people need that kind of help and GLIDE does such great work."

"Well, you know, it's the least I can do. We all need to do what we can to support those who need assistance. I've always tried to help others, but I like to do it in secret. I've been doing this work so long though, I'm becoming kind of famous, which is strange. It's funny, they're actually making a movie about me."

"Oh really?"

"Yeah, yeah, it should be good. Danny Glover, Billy Crystal and Robin Williams are all involved. Those three guys are real big into charity and when they heard what I do they thought it would be a great plot for a film. It's called 'Midnight Magic' and it's coming out sometime next year. It's almost done filming but we're missing an ending."

Down the street, I see the bus coming.

"That's awesome, I'll have to check it out. I'm going to have to get on the bus, but it's been really great talking to you."

Alan's face drops.

"Oh. Do you really have to go? It's been so nice to have someone to talk to. It's so hard finding people who just want to talk."

I'm not sure what prompted me to stay, probably some combination of guilt and a lack of hurry to start the day. I thought about how lonely it can be to get older and hoped someone humored my grandparents the same way at some time.

"Alright, just a few more minutes. I do need to get going soon though."

"I understand, everyone's very busy, rushing here and there. I'd be rushing too, but I ran into some trouble this morning."

"Oh no, what happened?"

"Well, in my rush earlier, I left my wallet and phone on the kitchen table, and I don't have any of my cash or cards on me. All I have are my keys. I'm not sure how I'm going to get my car out of Sutter/Stockton garage," he said, pulling a keyring out of his pocket.

"That's so frustrating. Maybe since they know you they can give you an IOU? Or you can try going into the bank?"

"Yeah, I don't know. It was a new guy today."

It's quiet for a few moments, until Alan says, "You know what would make a great ending to my movie?"

"What?"

"Well, I'm always helping people, right? What if at the end of the movie someone helps me?"

"Oh, I like that. That would be a good ending."

The 2 is a block away and it's getting later.

"Good luck with the movie, man. I'm sorry but I've really got to catch this bus."

"No, no, please. It's been such a pleasure to talk with you and you've inspired my ending! This is a big deal for me."

"I'm really sorry, I'm going to be late for work. I have to go."

"Ok, I'm going to try something. What if you lend me $30 to get my car out of the garage today, and tomorrow we can meet at 10:00 a.m. at the Chase Bank on Sutter and Montgomery, and I'll make it up to you?"

He gets more excited as he continues, "Yeah, yeah, this would be good! You can lend me the money and then I'll do one last good thing for you."

"I really like this ending, but I don't think I'm the person you're looking for."

"No, please. Please. You absolutely are."

The bus pulls up and the doors open. I take a step to board.

"Please, Kathleen, you're going to be sorry you missed this! You're giving up a great opportunity!"

I paused. *What am I doing? I'm going to be late. Why I have entertained this for as long as I have?* Another voice in my mind shot back—*who cares about being late? How many times have you showed up late or on time or early and it's made any significant difference? Who cares if you show up at all? Maybe there's more to life than—*

"Ma'am! Are you getting on the bus or not?"

"Oh. Um." I take a step down and wave the bus off. The driver rolls his eyes and the bus peels out of its lane.

"Ok, Alan. Make it good. What is this grand opportunity I'm missing work for?"

"Oh, you're going to be so glad you stuck around for this! Ok, so this is going to sound crazy but it will change your life, are you with me?"

"I'm with you. Try me."

"Ok, so, you lend me the money and then we meet tomorrow at Chase Bank at Montgomery. We'll go inside together and I'll wire $10 million dollars to your bank account. But, there are two things you have to do. These two things are very important to me, and you have to promise you'll do them. The first is you have to give $1 million to the homeless. Can you do that?"

"Yes, of course."

"Ok, good. The second thing is that if you ever make a movie or write a book about this encounter, that you not use my name. Like I said before, I don't do charity work for the publicity. Can you promise not to expose my identity to the public?"

"You got it."

"So, what do you say? You give me $30 and uphold two very easy promises, and I'll give you $10 million. And I'll get an end to my movie!"

I don't know what to think. The whole proposal is crazy. And I'm crazy. I'm standing around in 30-degree weather, talking to a random man. I've missed four busses, and I'm late for work. *What am I doing?*

For a moment, I allow my mind to wander.

Ten million dollars would change everything. Even $1 million would change everything. I could pay off my credit card, I could buy a house, I could really help others. I could go on a very long vacation. I wouldn't have to worry about money and watch how I spend. Maybe I should do it. It's crazy to think that one small decision could have such a terrific impact on my life, and suddenly I feel very possible. I thought I was just going to work, but I said yes to a stranger and now I'm being offered $10 million. Maybe my life isn't so much dictated by big life events, but more by tiny little moments. Maybe small choices are what determine how the larger ones are made. It's strange to think that every minuscule decision in my life has led me to this exact spot, at this exact time.

Throat clearing pulls me out of my thoughts, and I look up at Alan, who seems impatient. "Well, did you decide? This is a once in a lifetime offer."

"I realize that. It's just...it's a lot."

"Kathleen, if you can't see what an opportunity this is for you, for your family, an opportunity to help others—you DO want to help others don't you?"

"Yes, of course, I do."

"Of course you do. So, what is there to decide? You just say yes."

"I don't have cash on me, so I don't think I can do this. I don't think I can help."

"That's easy. You walk down to the ATM on the corner over there. You pull out the $30 and all of our problems are solved. If you can't see that I'm offering you a great opportunity, you're an idiot."

A chill comes over me. I stare across the street. *How does he know that there's an ATM over there?* I look down at my feet, my eyes pausing at Alan's hands as I lower my glance, and suddenly things feel like they're coming into focus. Alan's hands are dirty, and his nails are chipped and crusting. His suit jacket is missing a button, and his pants have faint stains. His shoes are scuffed up and I realize what many others would have already known by now: there is no $10 million, Alan was not raised by the Rat Pack, he's not a philanthropist and there's no "Midnight Magic" movie being made. Alan is a con man, and I am gullible, or maybe just anxious to believe that people are telling The Truth, and not just some fiction-based version of their own truth, stories they've been telling themselves and asking me to believe.

"Alan, I'm sorry. I can't help you today. I wish I could. I've left my wallet at home, so I don't have any money or cards." I pull my pockets out of my jacket to make the point.

He erupts. "You cannot be serious! I've been talking to you for what— 45 minutes? And you just now tell me you don't have any money?"

"I'm really sorry. Really."

He shakes his head at me. "You just wait. The bad things will catch up with you. Just wait."

He continues shaking his head, cursing me, my family, and anyone who ever has had or will have the displeasure of knowing me, as he walks off, looking back every few feet to wag a finger at me.

It's finally silent and I try to process the last hour of my life. I do feel bad for accidentally wasting his time. I know how frustrating it is to perform a dog and pony show in the hopes of making a sale, only to come up empty handed. To be vulnerable, and to be rejected.

But more than that, I feel free. When I left the house, I was half asleep, literally and figuratively, physically and existentially, but now, I feel awake, as if someone drenched me in ice water.

It's easy to sleepwalk through life, to not be intentional about where to spend time, or energy, especially when we are focused on just surviving. It's easy to feel emotional or mental paralysis, and to discount our own ability to create possibility or make choices, especially when living in a prison of our own making. And it's easy to confuse huge life milestones for living, when really, they're just roadside attractions in the midst of a journey.

I see Alan on my walk to work sometimes, looking older. I smile when I see him, silently thanking the snarling man for the $10 million lesson. I think he's still mad about the $30 though.

Grateful acknowledgment is offered to those that inspire me to write, fellow explorers and appreciators of absurdity, and most importantly, my parents, who have taught me that "there are eight million stories in the Naked City" and that beauty is all around us.

About the Author

Kathleen Emma is a writer and a lover. This is her first book.

About this Book

Safety Requires Avoiding Unnecessary Conversation is a true labor of love, and has been written over the past (almost) two decades. Since the first time she stepped foot into San Francisco, Kathleen has been impressed by how freely many artists share and distribute their work in San Francisco, and throughout the greater Bay Area. Now, more than ever, Kathleen believes that it is critical for art and writing to be accessible. These essays are her attempt to give back to this very special community. Although this book will be sold, it is not a for-profit effort. Any and all proceeds will be donated to 826 Valencia, a San Francisco-based nonprofit organization dedicated to supporting under-resourced students with their writing skills. For more information or to donate, please visit www.826valencia.org.